Wings of Meditation

by Harr-Joht Kaur Takhar

4

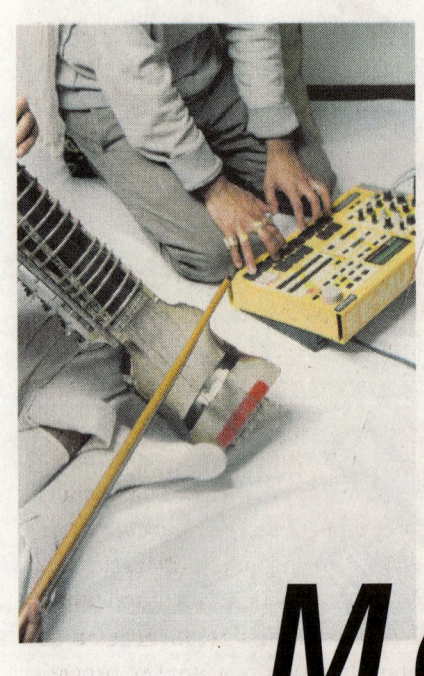

Photographs by Johanna Tagada, 2018

01

Petit Oiseau

music

Jatinder Singh Durhailay
&
Suren Seneviratne

Jatinder draws his bow. Suren hangs over his synth. The bow, sweeping across the Dilruba's strings, demands a controlled, steady hand. The drooped, nodding head responds to the seemingly scattered yet calculated finger movements which adjust the dials on the E-MU synthesiser. We observe such horizontal and vertical motions in relation to the seated positions of both performers. Suren's choice to play his tabletop synthesiser on the ground is unusual, yet deciding to meet his collaborator on the floor suggests his sensitivity to the demands of Indian classical music performance. It also establishes an equal playing field between the synthesiser, the Dilruba, Suren, Jatinder, and their audience.

The physical proximity of both musicians helps command an engaged audience – an essential ingredient of successful live music performance. Indeed, the listener's journey is accounted for by the meaning of the word 'Dilruba'; a Farsi word which roughly translates to 'stealer of the heart'. It suggests how the instrument's sound seizes and carries our very own emotional core with it. This notion of being carried certainly resonates with Jatinder's treatment of the instrument in Petit Oiseau. Sounds are swollen, expanded and layered, steadily unfolding through time. These smooth resonances are, however, also disrupted through Jatinder's attempts to imitate the synthesiser by plucking the smaller strings of the Dilruba. Though an unusual method to adopt, plucking demonstrates Jatinder's concern with creating an intimate dialogue between both instruments; one matched by Suren, whose compositions intermittently mimic the Dilruba through the synthesiser's palette.

Such exchanges, operating at a sonic level, are reified in this publication through measured textual and visual offerings. The choice to accompany a debut album with a design-led publication highlights how Petit Oiseau is not merely a musical project, but an artistic one too. Furthermore, it is a project which extends beyond the duo,

to the designer, editors and contributors who have materialised this vision. Petit Oiseau's music, composed and delivered by Jatinder Durhailay and Suren Seneviratne, of course lies at the nucleus of the project, and within this publication one will encounter material relating to their personal lives and influences. The most appropriate aspect to assess here are the snapshots extracted from the artists' family archives. These provide the most immediate link to the biographies of the pair and permits a reflection on the importance of the family archive itself.

Perusing a family photo album might accompany a shared nostalgia and sense of gratitude. Yet if one might struggle to answer, 'Where is home?', then unrecognisable elements encountered within the album may prompt a greater degree of questioning. Such enquiries can unfold into much wider discussions around cultural identity, migration and placemaking. I believe the family archive's strength lies in its ability to activate these otherwise silenced conversations and histories. Such prompts are necessary due to the shameful shortfalls of the British school syllabus. These shortfalls do not allow Jatinder, Suren, and indeed myself, to consolidate the dispiriting histories of colonialism, its implications on our heritage and its resonances on the now. Detangling this is a lengthy process, yet we should strive to utilise the family photo album – an underrated and invaluable tool.

The unadulterated strength of my grandparents to move to a Britain that presented persistent social strife and limited economic prospects is far beyond my comprehension. Yet this is something which I have relied upon my whole life. Jatinder's personal family archive contributions (p.14) support this expression of gratitude, as both images derive from his father's life in Ahmedabad and showcase the loving affinity shared between siblings. His father, Bhupinder Singh Durhailay, was born in Amritsar and travelled across

India and Sri Lanka extensively, before finally moving to London in 1973. In 1975 Bhupinder Singh married Parminder Kaur, who was one of many South Asian refugees escaping Uganda following Idi Amin's directive. Jatinder, as second-generation, has an arms-length relationship to the life and locations presented in these images, yet their appearance within this book serves to establish his proximity to them and close this gap.

The offerings from Suren's personal family archive (p.15) provide a more direct connection due to his status as first-generation. Suren was born in Kandy, arriving in London as a child in 1996. As he spent such a brief time in Sri Lanka, memories of his life out there are hazy and rose-tinted. The images demonstrate this, from joining his classmates in a playful protest-like gathering at school, to his assertive gaze and stance which proudly holds a guitar. As Suren moved to London, he transitioned from acoustic to digital forms of music production. This interest would organically germinate in South London, where UK Garage and pirate radio boomed in the nineties. The instrument Suren plays – an enchanting yellow edition of the E-MU XL-7 Command Station synthesiser from 2001 – interlinks with this period of expanded possibilities within electronic music. He stretches its intended use as a hip-hop synth, opting for a more minimalistic and ambient approach, which fuses more successfully with the Dilruba. This experimental approach is also born out of Suren's appetite to understand the more technical aspects of digital music engineering.

It is no surprise, then, that the sound generator for the Oramics machine is included within this publication (p.8). Imagined by Wiltshire-born Daphne Oram, co-founder of the BBC Radiophonic Workshop, the Oramics machine is a fascinating gem from the early experimental history of electronic music. It was developed by Oram in her Kent studio in 1957 and its audio signal was designed to match the composer's graphic notation. Electronic motors would process the waveform slides, annotated using brown ink, which then converted to sound. Another overlooked cultural figure who is also given space within this publication, is Kandy-born architect Minnette de Silva (p.12), a pioneer of Sri Lankan modernist architecture. De Silva studied at the Architectural Association from 1945 to 1948 and became the first elected Asian female associate of the Royal Institute of British Architects. She was committed to blending local craftsmanship traditions with the modernist styles she had familiarised herself with during her extensive travels.

Evidence of Sri Lanka's rich performance traditions are further presented through the inclusion of Kolam masks (p.10). A mask is adopted by each performer during Kolam ceremonies, a style of folk drama typically found on Sri Lanka's southern coast which features speech, dance and drums. Masks vary greatly in style but will often exhibit bright colours and exaggerated facial features. Further reference to local craftsmanship is embedded through Jatinder's illustrations of his instruments (p.16), which demonstrate how traditional artistry is preserved through design and ornamentation. For instance, the sound chamber of the Taus is elegantly formed by a peacock's body, which is firmly supported by its petite feet, and finely decorated through hand-painted embellishments and graceful carving. Jatinder's drawings indicate that his relationship to his instruments exists on both sonic and visual planes; an unsurprising concern considering his extensive artistic portfolio, which includes the continuation of the miniature-style painting tradition on handmade hemp paper.

Petit Oiseau cannot be anchored, which is proven by the wide-ranging content within this publication. The French title, translating to 'small bird', also suggests a resistance to be geographically placed. Indeed, cultural references to birds also span time and place, and once you search for them, they cannot be avoided. To end this introduction, I take this title as a starting point to outline how birds have entered my week, with an invitation for you to do the same.

7

Heard the occasional chirping of birds from out the window.

Farid ud-Din 'Attar's narrative poem Mantiq al-Tayr ('The Conference of the Birds') rests on my bookshelf.

Witnessed Pantha du Prince clad in a bird mask on stage, ending his performance with a plea to save the trees.

A low-flying pigeon prompted me to duck to avoid it in a London tube station.

Roots Manuva utters 'wings of meditation' on the radio in his feature on The Cinematic Orchestra's single, Caged Bird/Imitations of Life.

Daphne Oram

Oramics Machine

Waveform slide, one of two, part of the Oramics machine. Object number 2010-68/4 in the Science Museum's Collection.

Sound Generator, part of the Oramics machine.

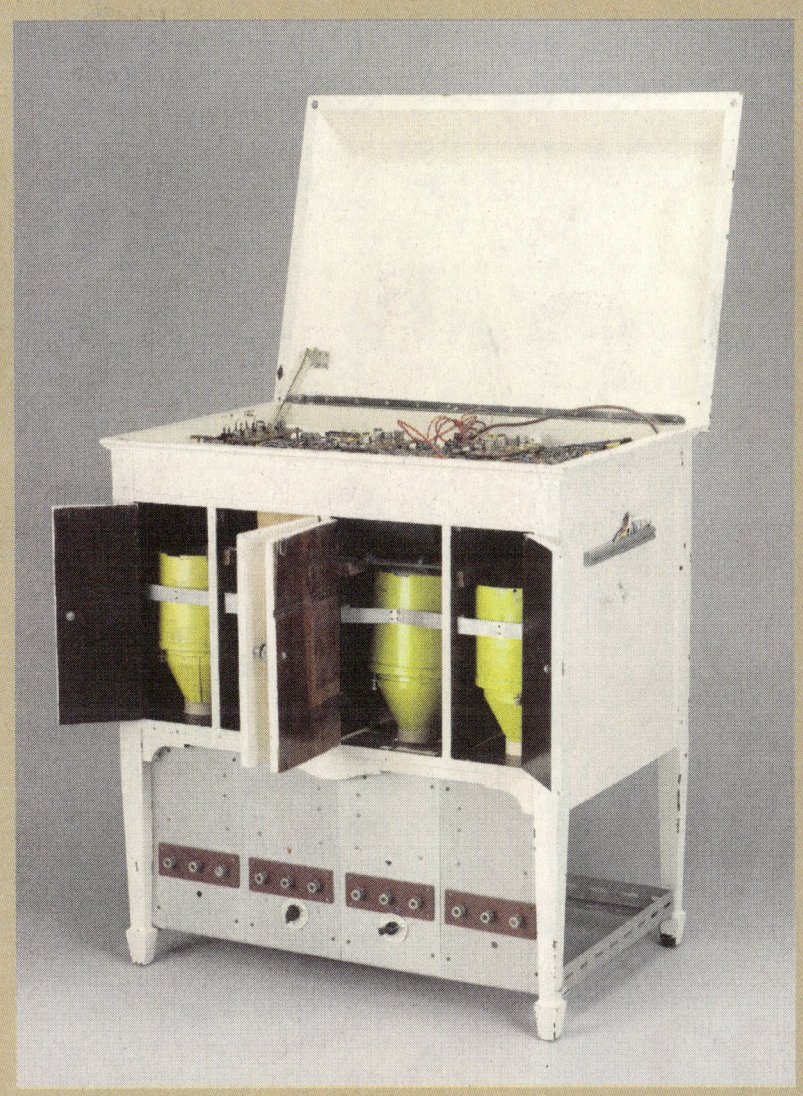

Measurements:
As displayed (lid open)
1267 mm x 755 mm x 516 mm
Type: synthesizer
Photographs courtesy of
The Science Museum, London.

kolam

These masks may have been used in Kolam performaces. These ritual performances were staged to appease the gods and demons, so that they would confer their blessings or heal the afflicted.

Kolam' literally means appearance or impersonation and it is thought that the plays began as an ancient fertility ritual. The plays may also be a prelude to the exorcism of demons, which are believed, in parts of Sri Lanka, to be the cause of disease.

10

This mask represents Heraya, the soldier from the Kolam play, his yellow face covered with cuts and sores, with leeches applied to them.

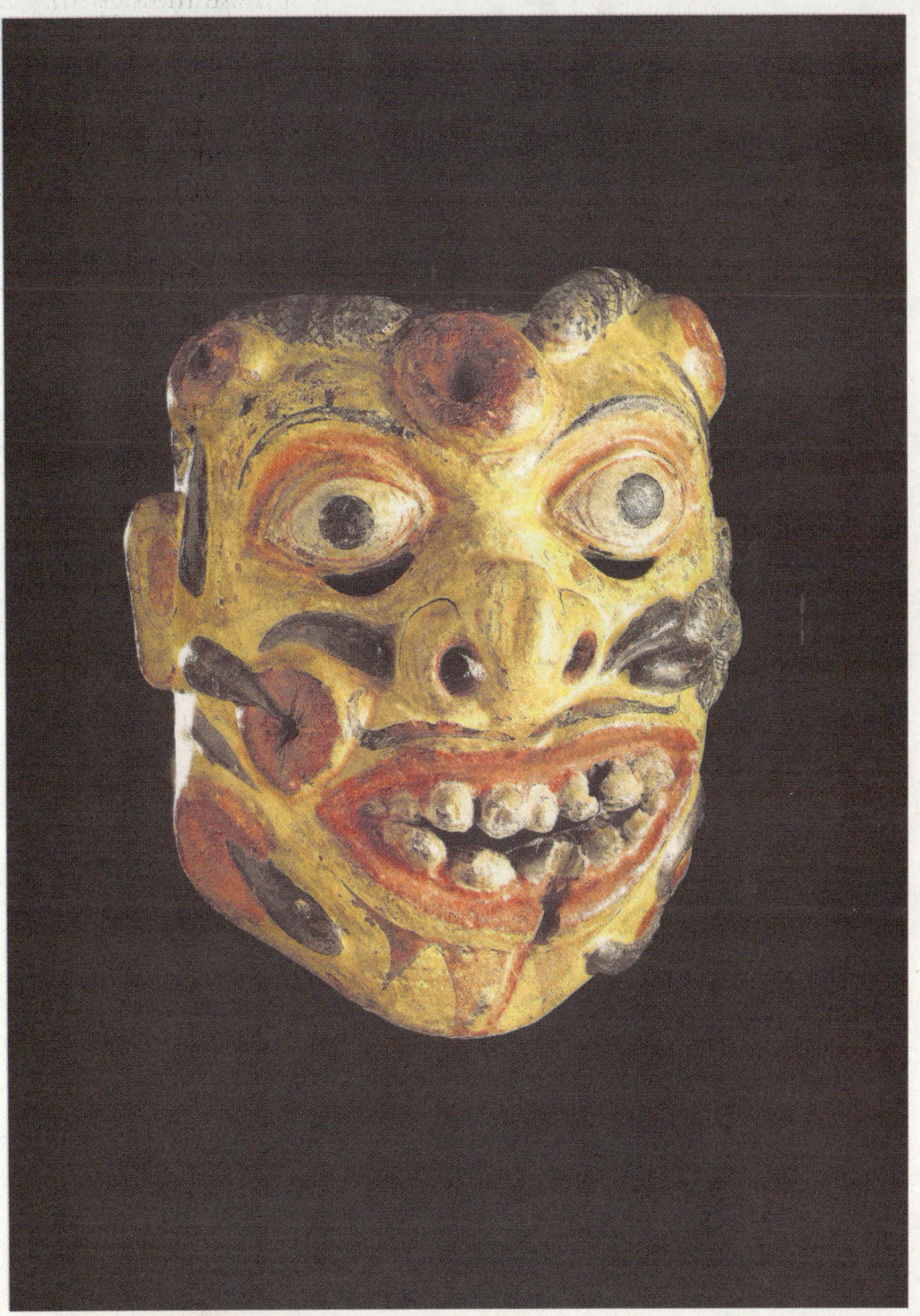

Covered in bites and leeches, this carved wooden mask represents Hevaya, the soldier from the masked kolam plays of Sri Lanka. There are over fifty characters in the plays and Hevaya represents a figure of fun.

Maker: Unknown
Location: Sri Lanka
Visuals and text courtesy of The Wellcome Collection, CC BY.

Minnette

1918
Born in Kandy, Ceylon.

1948
Ceylon gains independence as the Dominion of Ceylon.

1948
First woman to be trained as an architect and the first Asian woman to be elected an associate of the Royal Institute of British Architects (RIBA).

12

1996
Gold Medal by the Sri Lanka Institute of Architects.

1972
The Dominion of Ceylon becomes a republic, it is renamed the Republic of Sri Lanka.

1998
Dies in Kandy, Sri Lanka.

Illustrations by Jatinder Singh Durhailay

13

Karunaratne
House,
Kandy, 1951.

de Silva

MIGRATIONS

14

1) Jatinder's uncle *Chacha ji Parminder*.

2) Jatinder's dad *Bhupinder*.

Taken in India (location unknown), around 1960.

Taken in India (location unknown), around 1960.

1) Jatinder's aunt *Poaji-Rajinder* who lives in Punjab, India.

2) Jatinder's dad *Bhupinder* who lives in London, UK.

3) Jatinder's late uncle *Chacha-Moni*.

4) Jatinder's late uncle *Chacha-Perminder*.

Family Pictures

Suren (with headscarf) at École Internationale - School in Kandy, Sri Lanka, 1991.

Suren as a child in Sri Lanka.

Classical Indian

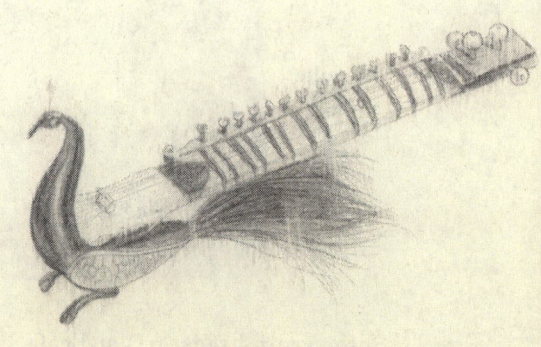

Taus

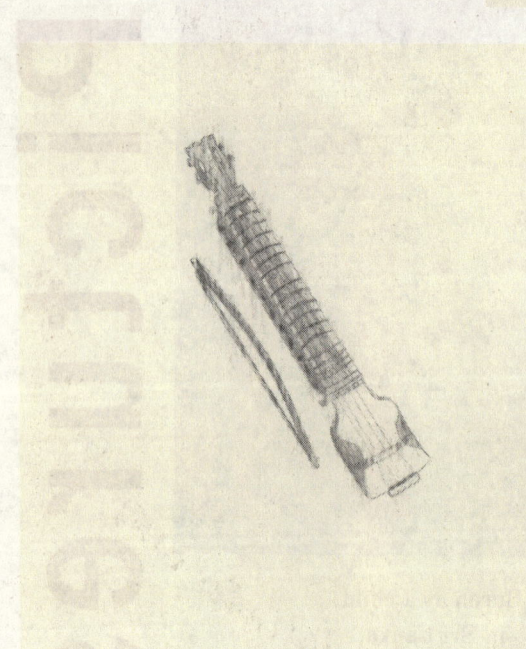

Dilruba

Instruments 17

Jori

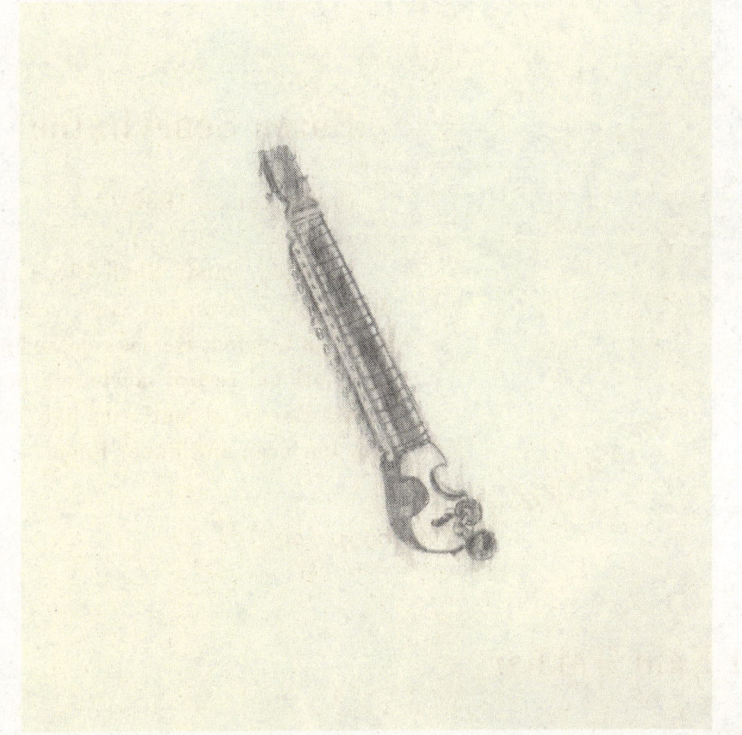

Tarshenai

Illustrations by Jatinder Singh Durhailay

Contributors

Jatinder Singh Durhailay

(b. UK, 1988)

is a painter, composer and musician born and based in London. Trained in the Indian classical singing art named Dhrupad, Jatinder plays the rare string instruments that are the Dilruba and Taus. He practiced thoroughly under the Hazuri Ragis in India, and Ustad Ranbir Singh in England. Durhailay's projects often combine sound and visuals, while juxtaposing with his interest for the lush and green jungles of India, as in *The Last Ballad of Mardana*. Exhibitions include *Inaka no Hana* at Nidi Gallery (Tokyo Japan) and *Empire Faith and War* at Brunei Gallery (London UK). Recent performances include The National Gallery (London UK) Maus Habitos (Lisbon Portugal), Vacant, and Atelier Fluss (Tokyo, Japan).

www.jatindersinghdurhailay.com

Suren Seneviratne

(b. Sri Lanka, 1986)

a.k.a My Panda Shall Fly, is a multi-disciplinary musician and sound artist based in London. He has released music on international record labels and performed across Europe at platforms like Tate Modern, Barbican and Boiler Room.

www.soundcloud.com/mpsf

Harr-Joht Kaur Takhar

(b. England, 1997)

graduated with a History of Art degree from the Courtauld Institute of Art. She is currently based in London, working extensively across arts, culture and heritage.

Johanna Tagada

(b. France, 1990)

is a painter and interdisciplinary artist based in London. Her practice composed of painting, drawing, photography, film, sculpture, installation, textile, writing and publishing is one that often conceals ecological messages rendered in soft and delicate methods. She is the founder of Poetic Pastel and co-founder of the publication series *Journal du Thé – Contemporary Tea Culture*.

www.johannatagada.net

Sarah Gissinger

(b. France, 1996)

recently graduated at DSAAD in Lyon with a degree in applied Arts - specialising in fashion and textile. She is presently Normalienne at École Normale Supérieure Paris-Saclay (Teachers' and Researchers' Training Higher Education School). Sarah's current research explores the possibilities that are considering and weighing our daily actions both as a constituent and contributor of the earth. This ongoing investigation is punctuated by constant back and forth between textile researches, creation of imagery, writing and editorial work.

www.sarahgissinger.fr

Tilmann S. Wendelstein

(b. Germany, 1980)

is an art director and designer and founder of the design studio 75W (Theory of a Small World). His life and work oscillate between Berlin and Tokyo from where he works for clients in Europe and Asia.

After studying graphic design in Germany he moved to Tokyo where he co-founded The Simple Society in 2010 which ran until 2018 with numerous awards and exhibitions along the way. He is the co-founder of the publication series *Journal du Thé – Contemporary Tea Culture*.

www.75w.studio

Poetic Pastel

is a positive and collaborative independent cultural project. In tune with the Deep Ecology movement and focusing on Art, Publishing and Textile. Poetic Pastel is an open conversation inspired by natural elements, warm memories, rhythm, colours, feelings, relationships, literature, poetry, tea culture and daily life. Poetic Pastel's projects result in exhibitions, gatherings, performances, writings, research, publications, contributions, textiles and quotidian objects. Through togetherness Poetic Pastel hopes to help restore respect for and appreciation of nature, while highlighting that humans are part of nature.

For a better world please say no to racism, discrimination, nukes, war, animal slaughter, sweatshops and pollution. Poetic Pastel encourages and supports the development of positive, cruelty free and sustainable lifestyles.

www.poeticpastel.com

A LIST ON HOW TO LOOK FOR CALMING SOUNDS IN THE CITY

GO UNDER A TREE WHEN IT RAINS

ENTER A LARGE SPACE

SEARCHING FOR ECHOES

WALK INTO A QUIET CHURCH

WAKE UP EARLY AND GO OPEN YOUR

EARS TO THE BIRDS IN THE PARK

DISCOVER THE LANGUAGES

AROUND THE CITY

LOOK FOR SILENCE

LISTEN TO YOUR OWN BREATH

by Petit Oiseau

Petit Oiseau
Jatinder Singh Durhailay &
Suren Seneviratne

Assistant Editor
Sarah Gissinger

Editorial Concept
&
Direction
Johanna Tagada

22

Essay
Harr-Joht Takhar

Proofreading
Harnam Kaur Chana

Newspaper Club

Printed by
Newspaper Club
in the United Kingdom

Art Direction
&
Design
T. S. Wendelstein
(75W)

Published by
Poetic Pastel Press
www.poeticpastel.com

Distribution and enquiries info@poeticpastel.com & hi@bonjourjohanna.com

First edition of 500 copies

Printed in October 2019

23

With special thanks to Simon Wright, MK Gallery, Juliette Riegel, Charan Singh Rattan, T. S. Wendelstein, Migrant Journal, The Church of Sound, The V&A Museum, Harry Singh Chana, The Design Museum, Senaka Weeraman.

With the support of Newspaper Club
www.newspaperclub.com

All rights reserved. No part of this publication may be reproduced or transmitted in any form or by any means, electronic or mechanical, including photocopying, recording or any other information storage or retrieval system, without prior permission in writing from the publisher.

Texts © the authors.
Images © Johanna Tagada, Wellcome Collection, Science Museum Group Collection
Copyright ©, Jatinder Singh Durhailay, the Durhailay and Seneviratne Families, Poetic Pastel Press 2019 and The Board of Trustees of the Science Museum.

music

PRESS

ISBN 978-1-5272-2961-7

Published by Poetic Pastel Press